Contents

Chapter 1: How to ruin your day

Congratulations! You woke up this morning, which means it's a perfect opportunity to turn an average day into an absolute catastrophe. You really have to start small to make the rest of your life as miserable mess. Like everything else you want to be good at, you need to focus on the small things. Ruining your day, every day, is the first and foremost goal you should do. If done correctly, you should be able to follow the rest of this book pretty easily.

In this chapter, we'll explore foolproof techniques to ensure you'll end the day thoroughly convinced that life is terrible—and it's all your fault. Ready? Let's dive in!

Step 1: Start Your Morning by Checking Your Phone

The first thing you do in your day is wake up. It should be an instant feeling of regret. You don't just start off by hating your life. You have to have something in your life that you hate. The thing that keeps you from depreciating your life is that you don't have much perspective on it. How can you possibly know what to complain about if you don't know how much better everyone else's life is?

Nothing says "good morning" like doomscrolling through bad news and social media feeds filled with other people's fake happiness. Compare your messy bedhead to your friend's meticulously curated vacation photos. Bonus points if you immediately regret every life decision you've ever made before brushing your teeth.

People who tend to have their life together will waste their mornings doing productive things. Some people believe that something as simple as starting off your day by making your bed can improve your approach to life. This is something you want to avoid completely.

You need to start off your day with a complete waste of time. Use the algorithms on your phone to dictate what you will be paying attention to. Phone addiction is very common in the first world, and causes people to be pretty miserable in the process. You really want to take advantage of the toxic environment of the internet.

Step 2: Skip Breakfast (or Just Have Coffee and Regret)

The first thing you might be tempted to do when you wake up is trying to have a balanced meal. Do not make this beginners mistake. So many people can increase their happiness with providing it with meaningless things like nutrients. Nutrients are what your body needs to produce adequate hormone levels throughout your day. They can also help repair damaged tissue. Meaning it could end your misery streak.

A miserable body is taken care of as little as possible. You need to have an increase of the hunger hormone to help with your anxiety.

Caffeine is a stimulant, but you probably are already addicted to it. Stimulants can have the negative benefits of increased heart rate, anxiety, increase in adrenaline, and can damage your internal organs without proper hydration.

Who needs a balanced meal when you can run on caffeine and a gnawing sense of inadequacy? Feel that jittery energy? That's the taste of impending dread! Don't worry, you'll crash before lunch, ensuring maximum crankiness.

Step 3: Overcommit to Tasks You Hate

Even if you appreciate your life, there are still things that you probably don't like doing with your valuable time. Time is very limited in the human lifespan. 80 years, or 960 months, or 4,160 weeks, or 29,120 days, or 698,880 hours, or 41,932,800 minutes, or 2,515,968,000 seconds are the advertised life expectancy of today. If you aren't careful, most of that time might be neutral time spent. Or enjoyable time if you aren't paying enough attention.

The trick, is to constantly be overwhelmed with the time that you do have. You really want things to feel like they are constantly rushing. Making plans is great, but that only gets you halfway there.

Say "yes" to everything—even things you know will make you miserable. Volunteered to organize Karen's office baby shower? Excellent! Signed up for a gym membership you'll never use? Perfect. Nothing says "self-destruction" like biting off more than you can chew. The time that you have is limited, so you need to work to hate it.

Step 4: Seek Out Petty Inconveniences

This might be difficult for some people. It usually takes someone who already has a decent bit of discontent in their lives to be able to pull it off. It really takes some familiarity with yourself to be able to find things to implicitly upset you. You need to really have an understanding of your usual environment. What is a petty inconvenience? It's something minor that doesn't really make your day bad by itself. It instead, reinforces a bad day you are already having.

. Being miserable is a lot like a 401K. You need to contribute small things to it over a long enough period of time for it to grow.

Stub your toe on purpose. Wear uncomfortable shoes. Stand in the longest line at the grocery store. Remember, a day filled with tiny frustrations is a day well wasted. If nothing else goes wrong, fret not—your phone battery is probably at 2%.

One of the best things you can do is driving on a busy road. With traffic preventing you from getting to a place you need to do to, you really will be fuming. Few people can resist the anger that is cause by a red light and a few thousand cars. Especially, if those other drivers don't know basic road etiquette. It really helps if you focus on how other, specific, drivers are the reason why your driving experience is so bad.

Step 5: Obsess Over Past Mistakes

The worst thing about life is that you will inevitably make mistakes. Those positive people will try to tell you things like, "it's a learning experience" or, "everyone makes mistakes." Not for our purposes. Shut those thoughts out of your head. You need to believe that you cannot learn anything from these mistakes other than your own inadequacies in life.

There is no feeling worse than hyper focusing on mistakes you make. Remember that awkward thing you said in middle school? Replay it in your head until your soul cringes. Remind yourself that everyone probably still remembers and judges you for it.

Prior mistakes are like a farm for negative emotions. And the beautiful thing is, they grow anywhere, and require little maintenance. They only need constant attention and thoughts surrounding them to maintain a good yield of misery in your life.

Step 6: Avoid Any Kind of Fresh Air or Sunshine

Vitamin D is considered to be one of the most important vitamins for happiness. Several studies have shown it to be very beneficial for your health and mood. Many people often take it in pill form because of this. You naturally get Vitamin D while standing in sunlight.

You know what else you get from sunlight? **Cancer.** Sunlight is overrated. Stay indoors, preferably in a dimly lit room. Bonus points if you can listen to a rainstorm on a loop to match the vibe of your inner turmoil.

You also avoid that feeling of breathing that fresh air. Why breath oxygen that smells like flowers, when you can have oxygen smell like dust? This makes it more likely to have some issues with indoor allergies. Constantly breathing in the same air over an over. You also can squeeze our more misery if you keep your living space unclean. That way, you have to smell the bad smells constantly.

Step 7: Interpret Neutral Comments as Personal Attacks

Nothing is as impersonal as it seems. Remember, communication is more than the words you use. Everything is full of tones, facial expressions, and clues to deeper meaning. You have to understand the subtext of the messages people send you. Remember, if you are staying negative, these subtexts will also be negative.

When your coworker says, "Nice job on the report," assume they're being sarcastic. When your friend says, "We should hang out soon," assume they mean "I feel obligated to say this, but I'd rather not." Paranoia is your best friend here.

Step 8: Procrastinate Like a Pro

Have an important task to do? Excellent. Avoid it at all costs. A "responsible" or "happy" person would probably tell you to get on top of that. They just want to share the toxic feeling of accomplishment with you. Don't let these people drag you up.

Time management can do only nothing but bring you comfort in life. It also can signal to other people that you are mature. You should avoid this at all cost. It is severely detrimental to you mental undoing.

Spend hours researching obscure trivia or reorganizing your sock drawer instead. The more looming the deadline, the better the eventual panic attack will be.

Step 9: Blow Small Problems Out of Proportion

Remember those minor inconveniences you've been practicing? It's time to expand on that. Remember that inconveniences are only half of the problem when it comes to overreactions. Reinforce the idea in your mind just how awful something is. You need to really get into the headspace that everything minorly wrong with the world is an afront to your life.

Spilled coffee on your shirt? Clearly, this is proof the universe is against you. Missed a call from your mom? Obviously, she'll never forgive you. Take every minor inconvenience and magnify it into a full-blown existential crisis.

Not panicking over your minor inconveniences is a serious lack of investment on your misery. You can still be miserable without it, but not as miserable as you could be. The appropriate reactions for minor inconveniences are as followed.

- Bursts of anger
- Crying

- Screaming in the air
- Asking "Why does this always happen to me?" Or something similar
- Blaming others who couldn't possibly have any control
- Feeling regret for your emotional weakness

Remember, you need to stay toxic. These reactions will be on full display for everyone else to see. This will help with a number of other contributions to misery that will come up later. Really remember to put on a show.

Step 10: End the Day with a 3 AM Existential Spiral

A complete lack of rest is the key to a miserable mind. The brain can only think logically if it has had adequate sleep. The brain will try to send you signals to go to bed, you must do everything in your power to ignore this feeling.

Why go to bed on time when you can stay awake pondering the meaninglessness of existence? Lie in bed scrolling through memes. This is very similar to step number one. Then suddenly remember you forgot to respond to an email from three days ago. Panic. Repeat. The increase in your stress levels will make sleep feel next to impossible.

To be your own worst enemy, you must think about every bad thing that has happened throughout your day. Let the racing thoughts prevent your bed from feeling comfortable. This way, you will yearn for the distraction of your phone.

This was a pretty comprehensive way of ruining your day. But your days are so limited. And you can only contribute so much into making one day as bad as possible. Let's start looking at options for how to think things into being a problem with: "The Art of Overthinking: A Masterclass in Paralysis"

Chapter 2: The Art of Overthinking: A Masterclass in Paralysis

Welcome to the fine art of overthinking, where a single thought transforms into an infinite loop of "what ifs" and "should haves." In this chapter, we'll teach you how to overanalyze every aspect of your life until you're immobilized by indecision. Why take action when you can drown in hypothetical scenarios?

Step 1: Turn Simple Decisions into Epic Dilemmas

Remember that there are always better options out there. You can never possibly know every conceivable option there is for you. It's always best to second guess yourself. And it's important to remind yourself that you are incapable of making the correct decision.

Is it time to buy a new phone? Well, not so fast! Spend hours comparing models, reading reviews, and debating whether you even deserve a new phone. You should probably interject your previously held guilt in this decision-making process. Any decision you have can be a new opportunity for some existential dread.

A good thing to think over would be something akin to what kind of car you are trying to buy. Remember, there is always further issues with your decisions down the road. If you need to buy a car, you have to consider the mileage, what kind of gas does it take how new the car is, whether or not you like the car, and whether it is within your budget. You can even go a step further and think of the pollution you will be contributing by driving it. Not to mention the fact that you have to get insurance with it. That's an entirely new process for decision making right there.

Buying a car is a rare and expensive example though. Perhaps you can't buy a car every day. You are probably broke after all. Let's take a more common example. What kind of food to eat? Deciding what to eat can be an entirely complex interaction of guilt, desire, affordability, and your general view of yourself. If you eat healthy, you probably really want something bad for you. In this case, you can feel guilty for even thinking of breaking the diet you worked so hard for.

If you eat really bad, then you should consider that you're the product of what you eat. Garbage in, garbage out. And because you eat garbage, you are garbage. You should really consider wanting to eat healthy, without having the will power to do so. That way, every meal will be followed by an endless guilt. A guilt that you simply cannot change your current circumstance.

Step 2: Rethink Every Past Decision

Why just stop at making the decisions themselves as stressful as possible? Remember how you've been focusing on your previous mistakes? You can do the same things with your decisions. Every decision you have ever made can be an endless source of misery.

Remember that time you ordered chicken instead of fish three years ago? Let's revisit that choice. Was it the right call? Would your life be different if you had gone with the fish? Probably not, but let's stew on it anyway—just in case.

You have to highlight every facet of your decision making possible. Make sure that you correlate your prior decisions to your current situation. A common decision that many people stress about is their careers. Careers are the bedrock of how your life is going to be. And if you give yourself a time limit, then your choice it too late.

Step 3: Assume You're Psychic

Every interaction holds hidden layers of meaning that only you can decode. Remember that your actions are always to be in other people's thoughts. Every time you judge someone else, they are going to do the same thing with you. You can tell when you're obviously lying about what you think about someone else. Don't you think they can do the same thing back?

Really focus on the minutia of what other people are saying. What are their facial expressions? What is their tone? Do they have the same reasons for not liking you that you do? Remember, if you hate yourself, other people will likely hate you too.

Did your friend text "okay" instead of "OK"? Clearly, they're upset. Did your boss say, "Can we talk tomorrow?" Obviously, you're getting fired. That one is similar to a significant other telling you, "We need to talk." They are obviously cheating on you.

Congratulations, you're now a mind reader—and it's ruining your life.

Step 4: Ask "What If" Until You Break

The best question you can ask yourself to maintain your misery is, "What if?" The prior decisions that you made can continuously haunt you by adding this simple task continuously throughout your life.

- What if you make the wrong choice?

- What if people judge you?
- What if your friends or family don't like you?
- What if you're really bad at the things you like?
- What if people find you annoying?

Ask these questions repeatedly, preferably while staring at the ceiling at 2 AM. Let them spiral until the absurdity reaches critical mass and you're convinced your entire existence is a sham. Remember that the best person to gaslight you is always going to be yourself.

Step 5: Research Pointless Things

People often recommend that you should continuously educate yourself. Learning is supposed to be the best tool for improving your life. It can also be an amazing tool to help ruin your life. Remember that useful education might actually help you change your current situation.

How do you use learning things to make your life worse? It's quite simple actually. Instead of spending time learning a skill, learning how to be a better person, or learning how to be kinder to yourself, you should waste your time learning about the most random topics you can find. The more useless the information the better.

Got a question about how microwaves work? Spend three hours on Wikipedia learning about magnetrons. Will this knowledge improve your life? Probably not. But it's the perfect distraction from actually dealing with your problems.

Remember, you are trying to give yourself a temporary feeling of accomplishment. The feeling of accomplishing something will only be temporary, so you won't have to ruin your terrible mood. The feeling of completely wasting your time will more than make up for the feeling of learning something. Remember, accomplishment without result, will lead to long term mental unhealth.

Step 6: Plan for Every Worst-Case Scenario

This one is very similar to step two. Only now, you really need to lean into the what ifs of the world around you. The key to this is that no idea is off limits. You can think of any worst-case scenario that your brain will let you. Before making any decision, list every possible thing that could go wrong. Let these catastrophes play out in your head until you decide it's safer to do nothing.

Let's say you want to go somewhere that has a lot of people. If you really think about it enough, other people can be dangerous. There are criminals and crazy people out there. You need to consider that the risk of being mugged wouldn't be worth it. Even if it's a somewhat small chance. You need to plan out your route, have enough people with you, maybe even bring a gun with you.

Or you want to ask someone for something. Maybe, your boss. You could ask for that raise, but what if they get mad at you? What if they start to think that you are unhappy with your job? What if you actually make more money than everyone else, and you're just bad with your money?

There truly is no possible limit. Especially if you are paranoid. Then you can have some wild theories about aliens finding you. Always remember that a prepared mind is a scared mind. And fear will simply prevent you from enjoying your life. Stay at home to do the same things you always do.

Step 7: Seek Advice, Then Ignore It

Now that you've probably had some severe anxiety, it's time to make it other people's problem. Any friends or family you actually have will likely be worried about you. People who are worried about you will probably try to get you to talk about your problems. This would be a good time to open up. But, opening up and receiving advice would go against our goals. So, you need to ignore that advice. That way, you can continuously experience the feeling of making someone feel bad for you without actually solving your problems.

Ask five different people for their opinions, then disregard everything they say. Instead, focus on how their answers contradict each other and conclude that no one understands your situation—not even you. Remember, you can twist anything to be meaningless with enough effort.

This process helps you to justify your own thinking to yourself. You need to be completely convinced that the subject is just too complicated for people to really grasp. They might even suggest taking medication to help with it. Medication is unnatural, and you should probably just learn how to deal with your mental health issues in your own way.

This will amplify your problems. You will naturally spiral into a more chaotic and unstable person. Given enough time, people will eventually leave you alone. Being alone is good for your mental unbeing. It gives you less ways of dealing with your stress, and more ways to wonder why people don't like you. Eventually, you can just accept the idea that you are too broken to be fixed.

Step 8: Use Google to Confirm Your Fears

Remember that mental health is a complicated subject. The best way to make your mental health worse, is by simply researching it yourself. Nearly every action or habit you have can be traced to some previously established mental illness. This way, you can think something is mentally wrong with you without actually knowing.

The same thing could be said about your physical health, or nearly everything else. Got a weird symptom? Google it and convince yourself you have a rare and incurable disease. Need reassurance about a financial decision? Google horror stories of people who lost everything.

The internet is your best friend when it comes to amplifying paranoia. Any opinion you have can simply be justified by looking in the right places. It simultaneously has the most information, and misinformation. Any decision from seeking professional help, to making financial decisions can be made worse because of your, "research." It's important to remember that the term research is a placeholder for confirming previously established fears.

Step 9: Avoid Making Decisions Altogether

By now, you should be an anxious mess. Your thought process is so screwed up that you need to really think about everything until you convince yourself to not go through with anything. Your own pressure that you created will be a constant echo of misery.

What you will be witnessing is putting in a lot of work to accomplish absolutely nothing. This way, you will only be left with the stress that you caused. Ambition is the enemy of misery. You can teach yourself to not want anything out of life.

Why choose when you can just... not? Let indecision become your default setting. Sure, you'll stay stuck, but at least you won't make any mistakes. Paralysis is just another word for stability, right?

Now that you feel pretty self-conscious about your life choices, let's take it a step further. Why just worry about your choices? Comparing yourself to others is way more toxic in the next Chapter: "Comparing Yourself to Others: Because You're Definitely not Good Enough"

Chapter 3: Comparing Yourself to Others: Because You're Definitely Not Good Enough

Ah, comparison—the thief of joy and the best way to confirm that you'll never measure up. Why settle for self-acceptance when you can scroll endlessly through lives that seem infinitely better than yours? In this chapter, we'll guide you through the art of tearing yourself down by holding a magnifying glass to everyone else's highlight reel.

Step 1: Start Your Day with Social Media

Wake up, roll over, and immediately grab your phone. Instagram, TikTok, Facebook—it doesn't matter.

Feast your eyes on vacation photos, perfect family portraits, and influencers drinking smoothies that cost more than your entire grocery budget. Let the comparison sink in before your feet even hit the floor.

The name of the game is complete comparison to your own life. Nearly everyone that shares your hobbies, interests, career choices, and goals can probably do it better than you. You need an initial exposure to just how shitty you're doing in life. You really want to avoid any doomscrolling that shows how much better your life is than the third world.

Instead of just randomly doomscrolling, here are some tips for the types of people to follow. The first one is gym influencers. Most of them have entire careers of selling you products that don't work. Many of them take performance enhancing drugs to help maintain their careers. And they can't really reveal that to you. Most of the time, they will simply tell you that you need to work harder to look like them. This way, you can commit to a health goal that might be physically impossible for you.

Another very popular option is business savvy people. People who seem to just have a lot of money, but don't really do anything but talk about how hard they worked for it. Their entire personas are based on the idea that they have more than you. And similarly, to the fitness influencer, they tell you it's because you simply don't work hard enough. They may even go so far as making sure you get to see the luxury things they've bought with their money. This way, you have someone you can compare your cheaper items to.

There are countless examples of people you can look at on the internet to put you on the path of misery. There are also many examples of things you should avoid. Try to avoid doing these things with your phone when doomscrolling.

- Talking with loved ones
- Checking your responsibilities
- Planning your day

- Looking at people with worse situations than you

These are examples of things that you might end up looking forward to. Things that can decrease your stress levels and make you feel lucky to be alive. They also might end up giving you organized goals to accomplish. Accomplishing these can be toxic to your misery.

Step 2: Compare Your Worst to Their Best

People will try to tell you that you are capable of doing great things. People will try to tell you that you are only going through a rough patch in life. You should do everything in your power to ignore these people. Your previous obsession with your own mistakes should constantly be a reminder of your failures in life.

When you're at your lowest, remind yourself that someone out there just won an award, got engaged, or bought a house. Sure, you're eating cereal for dinner again, but that's no reason to cut yourself any slack. You need to fixate on how much more perfect other people's lives are.

It's not like they're struggling with anything—they're perfect, obviously. And the only reason why you struggle so much is because you are so very flawed as a person. You also have to forget the notion that people are controlling what you see in social media. Examples of things that are constantly faked on social media are as follow.

- Physiques
- Lavish lifestyles
- Career's
- Intelligence
- Opinions

You really want to avoid the fact that many of these things you find in other people's internet personas are just fake. Just have that thought completely leavy your mind entirely.

Step 3: Assume Everyone's Success Came Effortlessly

Remember that you worked so very hard for everything. You were there, you experienced your life, you know the hard days you had. Now, just think about the people who had it better than you. They were probably just lucky. That coworker who got a promotion? Clearly, it wasn't due to hard work. They're just lucky. Your college friend's new business? Probably inherited money. Their success has nothing to do with effort—and everything to do with how unfair life is.

You have to remind yourself how unfair life is. Don't pay any attention to how someone might have reached their goaled. It's much easier to dismiss their success as just being born lucky. And you were born unlucky. Luck is a skill that you just can't really seem to maintain.

Really think about how bad things just seem to happen to you. And good things just happen to other people. You need to remember the amount of effort you put into things. Don't think about that too hard though. Remember, you don't want to be in a headspace where you can consider that someone else also worked hard. They were just in the right place at the right time. And they won the genetic lottery.

Step 4: Magnify Your Flaws

Understand that you are a very flawed person. Mentally ill people constantly focus on what's wrong with them. It's almost like they don't want to feel comfortable in their own bodies. A sixth sense that tells you that you are wrong. Every blemish, scar, skin irritation, tan line, and hair out of place is just one more thing wrong with you that needs to be fixed.

You also can look at other things about yourself that goes beyond just your physical appearance. Real narcissistic, miserable people can fixate on nearly anything about their personality that they can just really hate on. They are good at justifying their own self-hatred so much that they hardly need a good reason to not like themselves.

Find one thing about yourself you dislike, and obsess over it. Your hair isn't shiny enough. Your laugh is weird. Your handwriting looks like a deranged chicken's. Focus on these tiny imperfections until they feel like insurmountable character flaws.

Don't let those toxically positive people ruin your own terrible mood by telling you that nobody else really notices those flaws. Or that they aren't that important. They will try to cheer you up by showing you that it's not that big a deal. You need to focus on it so much that your borderline obsessed over it.

Some important things to ignore when getting into this headspace would include things like

- Acknowledging that it's not that big of a deal
- Realizing that everyone has minor flaws

- Realizing that some people have it worse than you do

Things like this just get in the way of you appropriately being toxic in life. A flawed person can only remain flawed if they focus on their problems, without working on their problems. Leave these issues about yourself alone until they become a sensitive topic to you.

Step 5: Keep a Mental Scoreboard

You need to have concrete reasons as to why you are dissatisfied with yourself. Since you are already comparing yourself to unrealistic people, how about more realistic people. The people around you are always going to be better than you at something. You need to fixate on the things that they are better at than you.

Turn life into a competition where you're always losing. They've traveled to more countries. They have more followers. They've learned five languages while you're still struggling with your native one. The scoreboard doesn't lie: You're losing at life.

This is a more relatable way of hating yourself. People being marginally better than you at things can be more hurtful that people who are way better than you at things. It's hard to connect to the idea that a 3-year-old plays an instrument better than you. You might feel a little bummed out by their youthful talents, but everyone knows that it's an extreme example.

Take that same idea, and think of a friend that's better than you at something. This is more personal and relatable. It eats away at you a little more by the sheer fact that it's a more attainable goal to reach. The fact that you know it's possible for you to improve enough to be better makes it hurt more.

Or you can look at things that you have never been good at. Like, making a room laugh at your jokes. You ever been in that situation? You say a joke, to almost no reaction. Then someone else says something similar and everyone is rolling on the ground laughing? That's because they have something you don't have. An actual sense of humor. This is something that is not so easily learned, but everyone would love to have.

Step 6: Ignore Context Completely

The most dangerous thing to your mental undoing could be understanding that someone isn't as awesome as they claim to be. Context can give you insight that would make it pretty difficult to brood about them. It's important to understand that everyone has struggles they go through to get to where they are. And they might have consequences that are worse than yours.

When someone posts a picture of their new car, assume they're living a stress-free life. Forget that they might be drowning in debt. Context is for optimists. Focus only on the shiny, happy exterior. Avoid the reality that people might actually be facing for once.

The art of pessimism is a sacred and traditional way of discrediting yourself. You lack of a happy exterior is a reflection of your inner feelings. You portray your sadness openly. So, people who seem happy must actually be happy. Otherwise, you wouldn't feel so bad for not being them.

Step 7: Compare Apples to Oranges (and Feel Bad Anyway)

The inverse of people who you can relate to, are people who have nothing to do with what you are feeling bad about. Every area of life has people who are amazing at it. But, why stop at comparing yourself in the same subject?

People live completely different lives from each other. If you can ignore that someone's circumstance can contribute to their abilities, then you can feel bad for not being able to replicate their lives. If you work a full-time job, you can be envious of someone who has a lot more free-time to work out.

Are you an artist comparing yourself to a tech mogul? A parent comparing yourself to a world traveler? Perfect! Comparing completely different lives is an advanced technique in self-sabotage. Make sure to ask yourself, "Why am I not doing all of those things simultaneously?"

You really want to treat yourself like you have the capability of always doing more. Even if you cannot possibly fit more into your busy schedule. The illusion of time is a pretty good excuse to be harder on yourself. People who are successful will say things like

- Sleep faster
- Take an Hour a Day
- Utilize your time management
- There is no excuse

If you forget that these people were in very particular situations to get to where they are, you can just blame yourself for not being there. Realistic expectations of your life will be the downfall of your doom and gloom mentality. Always set yourself up for disappointment.

Step 8: Envy People You Don't Even Like

You don't need to admire someone to compare yourself to them. You can compare yourself to people that you never even cared for. That high school frenemy? Sure, they're insufferable, but their Instagram grid is flawless. Spend hours wondering why the universe rewards such obnoxious people.

Your perception of them will move your mind into thinking that they are undeserving. Even if they haven't really lived the same life as you. You can let these people occupy parts of your consciousness. The very idea of them will feed onto your personality.

You can even go so far as obsessively keeping track of their current dilemma. Stalk them on the internet so you can savor when they are going through a hard time. Or, you can be envious of their lives being perfectly fine while you spiral out of control.

Making other people's business is your business. Sure, you don't get paid with money. Money is an afterthought. In fact, it's probably for the worst that you don't get paid for keeping track of these people. As long as you have contempt for them, you will find reasons to include them into your life. Ironically, you might even spend more time on people you don't like than your actual friends. Now you're letting yourself be miserable!

Step 9: Make It All About You

Nobody else is allowed to have anything good in their lives if you have anything to say about it. Be the gloomy person that has to constantly remind people that your situation is worse than theirs. Someone else having a good thing shouldn't have to get in the way of your bad time.

When a friend shares good news, find a way to feel bad about it. They got a new job? Great—remind yourself that your career is stagnant. They're expecting a baby? Cool—contemplate your lack of direction. Their happiness is clearly a reflection of your inadequacy.

It's important that you have outlets to reinforce your crappy attitude. Everything has to revolve around your problems. If you cannot focus on your own issues when other people speak to you, then you just aren't cut out for being miserable. Your misery requires you to be in the correct headspace 24/7. You need to show other people your skills in seeing the bad in your situations.

Step 10: Rinse and Repeat

Comparing yourself to others is one of the fundamental skills that miserable people are capable of. You should never celebrate who you are as a person. You should always be filled with shame, embarrassment, and discouragement from the people around you. These are important for a negative headspace.

In this chapter, we discussed the various outlets that you have to compare yourself to others. Your options are nearly limitless, especially if you utilize your internet connections. Nearly every facet of your life can be shown with better examples with other people.

When you've exhausted all the people in your immediate circle, move on to strangers. Celebrities, influencers, random people on LinkedIn—it doesn't matter. There's always someone more successful, attractive, or accomplished to compare yourself to.

And there you have it: a foolproof guide to feeling inadequate! By mastering the art of comparison, you'll ensure that no accomplishment or moment of joy goes untainted. Up next: "Procrastination: Why Do Today What You Can Cry About Tomorrow?"

Chapter 4: Procrastination: Why Do Today What You Can Cry About Tomorrow?

Ah, procrastination—the fine art of doing absolutely everything except the thing you're supposed to be doing. Why dive into productive work when you can postpone it indefinitely and enjoy the mounting pressure of an impending deadline? In this chapter, we'll explore how to master the delicate balance of avoidance, denial, and last-minute panic.

Step 1: Redefine "Priorities"

Priorities are a great way to understand what is important in your day. If you have your priorities straight, you might end up being satisfied with yourself. Look at what you have to do with your day. Think of the long term positive impact you can accidentally give yourself if you go out of your way to be responsible.

When faced with a crucial task, ask yourself: *Is this really more important than alphabetizing my spice rack?* Spoiler: It's not. Nothing says "I'm in control" like meticulously organizing your pantry while your actual responsibilities scream for attention.

Postponing things that are important is a great way to add stress in your life. You should constantly feel as though you are in a rush of some sort. Battling with the counting down of minutes until you have no choice but to hurry.

Step 2: Set Unrealistic Goals

Part of being irresponsible is by making sure any task you want to accomplish is impossible. You need to have goals but look for things with an unrealistic standard. Things take time and patience. Those are things that healthy people have. And you aren't healthy. You need to impatiently approach what you want so you can sabotage yourself.

Overwhelm yourself by deciding to tackle the entire project in one sitting. Ignore the idea of breaking it into smaller, manageable tasks. The best way to do nothing is to convince yourself that doing anything is too much.

If you want to be healthier, just overcomplicate it. You have to have the perfect program, perfect diet, and perfect body. Learn everything you can about it until you are too mentally exhausted to even start. You should try to start at the finish line, instead of taking the race towards your goals one step at a time.

Step 3: Embrace Distractions

I absolutely love distractions. And today's technology makes it easier than ever to constantly have something pulling at your attention. You should be filling your entire house with useless technology that's specifically designed to have your eyes look at it as much as humanly possible. Cell phones, video games, computers, televisions, there's no real limit to having things ruin your goals by distracting you.

Did you know that now is the perfect time to deep-dive into obscure Wikipedia articles or binge-watch an entire season of a show you're not even that interested in? Procrastination thrives on the idea that there's always something more entertaining than the task at hand.

Maybe you want to be old school. Technology might not be your thing. You can have a good old-fashioned hobby. Or a million hobbies at the same time. Things that constantly need you to focus yourself on them instead of actually improving on yourself. Remember to only use it as a distraction from your problems so that it doesn't give you any fulfillment.

Step 4: Convince Yourself You Work Best Under Pressure

Why start early when you can wait until the absolute last minute? Sure, the stress will be unbearable, and you'll probably cry, but it's all worth it for that sweet, sweet adrenaline rush. Deadlines are just suggestions… until they're not.

The countdown that you will constantly have will put your body in a constant state of anxiety. You need to race against the clock to get everything done. If you have four months to do something, that should mean that you have three months and twenty-nine days of doing nothing before you even start. Last minute work is the best way to not enjoy your work, and improve your stress levels.

Step 5: Overprepare to Avoid Starting

You never can fully understand enough to start something. Research should cover the gaps in your knowledge. A normal person will do some research to get a better understanding of what they need to do, or if they are interested in that particular action. You want to take this thinking to the absolute limit.

Need to write a report? Spend hours researching, outlining, and designing the perfect color-coded spreadsheet. Tell yourself you're being productive, even though you haven't actually done any of the real work yet.

The over-preparedness of your research will cause you to eventually give up. All of that research will make it to where you will be completely discouraged from the even thought of starting a new project or improving something. Everyone on the internet will give you more information than you can physically handle. You should listen to them when they tell you that you haven't researched enough on a subject.

Step 6: Rationalize Your Avoidance

If you follow these steps enough, you might have a lapse in your illogic. You might recognize that you are irrationally making your life worse by deliberately taking negative actions. You need to silence these thoughts. You are too smart for your brain to fool you into thinking that you could ever be wrong. You need to justify your actions to yourself.

Rationality can be the double-edged knife that you are looking for. You can use that big brain of yours to think of reasons as to why you didn't start that thing you were supposed to do. Rationality is a tool, and it can be abused.

Create elaborate excuses for why you can't start. *I'm too tired. I'll have more energy tomorrow. Mercury is in retrograde.* Whatever the reason, the key is to make it sound plausible enough to justify another day of doing nothing.

Step 7: Reward Yourself Prematurely

You still might take small steps towards actually accomplishing something. There is a solution to this problem too. You can de-motivate yourself by rewarding any minor action you take. If you didn't clean, but took the trash out, then you deserve a cookie. All of your minimal actions can be stopping points for larger actions if you just get too full of yourself.

Tell yourself you've earned a break before you've even started. *I'll begin after one episode… or two… or the entire series.* Remember, it's important to stay well-rested for the task you're actively avoiding.

The best thing you can do this with is any diet you are trying to have. Instead of being lame and consistent with your food, remember that it is a calorie in, calories out math problem. That salad wasn't something metabolically healthy that could replace an otherwise bad meal. Those were good calories. And you deserve those bad calories as a reward. You can even give yourself a snack or five for doing a minimal amount of exercise.

Step 8: Make a To-Do List You'll Never Use

The concept of accomplishing something will always be more important than actually accomplishing something. You want to find things that make you feel like you're doing something. And setting up the idea of the work is the only part of the job that you are going to do.

Write down everything you need to do, then place the list somewhere you'll never look at it again. Making a list of something puts you in the mindset that you are going to do something. All you have to do is not follow the list.

You probably should use the out of sight, out of mind principle. Put the list somewhere that you might notice it on occasion. That way you notice it but forget to follow it by the time a few moments pass. Instead of putting it on the fridge, you should put it on a table. Somewhere where there is a lot of traffic for random things. That way it'll blend in.

Step 9: Spiral Into Guilt

If all tasks have been followed accordingly, you should have a lot of things set up that you haven't done. It's a constant cycle of setting up work, not doing anything, pushing things off until the last minute, and wondering where it all went wrong. The artform will work pretty quickly to make you miserable.

After hours (or days) of avoiding your task, let the crushing guilt of wasted time set in. This is a critical step in the procrastination process. Make sure to beat yourself up about it just enough to feel bad, but not enough to actually start working.

This puts you in a constant state of setting your mind up for success, and constantly failing. It puts you in a pretty extreme emotional roller coaster. This is very unhealthy for normal people. Normal people are fully capable of having some responsibility. These steps will surely make you a professional depressed doomer.

Step 10: Panic and Scramble at the Last Minute

Procrastination has now set you up to the last minute. The fatal moments where everything has to be done. Normally, the tasks start to fall apart. Nothing can be done well. But you had all of this time to enjoy yourself instead of getting work done ahead.

When the deadline finally arrives, channel all your anxiety into a frantic burst of productivity. Sure, it won't be your best work, and you'll lose several hours of sleep, but at least it'll be done… kind of.

You will leave your tasks to be half completed, or not completed at all. You'll be asking your boss or teacher for an extension on that assignment. And because this is your normal spiral, you will most likely have already had multiple chances beforehand. Now, your superiors don't trust you. This will contribute to much lower self-esteem than you had previously. Really giving you something to frown about.

Procrastination is an art form, and with enough practice, you can become a true virtuoso. Why rush to accomplish something when you can savor the exquisite torment of waiting until the last possible second? Next up: "Sleep is for the Functional: Perfecting the 3 AM Spiral."

Chapter 5: Sleep Is for the Functional: Perfecting the 3 AM Spiral

Ah, the 3 AM spiral. It's not just a passing moment of self-reflection; it's an art form, a ritual that transforms the quiet, peaceful hours of the night into a chaotic internal monologue. While the "functional" people are sound asleep, blissfully unaware of the impending chaos, you are awake, reflecting on the deep and meaningful questions of life—questions that, at 3 AM, you can't escape. Why does life even exist? What is the meaning of all this? Did I leave the oven on? Can I still make a career out of my hobby of rewatching TV shows? Congratulations! You're about to perfect this unholy process and turn it into an existential crisis that will make the next day feel like a marathon in quicksand.

Step 1: Set the Scene for Maximum Anxiety

To achieve the full power of the 3 AM spiral, it's important to set the right atmosphere. Ensure the lights are off, the world is quiet, and you're lying in a completely still position, with nothing but your thoughts and the growing sense that you're spiraling into madness.

Bonus points if you've recently scrolled through social media or watched a documentary on climate change, because nothing sparks a deep, irrational panic quite like knowing you're part of a doomed species. If the house is quiet and there's an eerie, distant sound of crickets outside, you're all set for the perfect storm. You're not just lying in bed—you're preparing for an internal showdown of epic proportions.

Remember that you really need to have set up your day for maximum anxiety. Caffeine should always be consumed to make sure you can't properly sleep. It is the best tool in your arsenal to increase stress and cortisol levels.

Step 2: Begin with Small, Innocent Thoughts

The beauty of the 3 AM spiral is how it starts innocently. You might begin by simply reflecting on the day—"Hmm, I wonder why I didn't get that email back." And just like that, you've launched yourself into a sea of questions, with no real answers in sight.

Maybe you'll think about that embarrassing thing you said last week, and then you'll spiral into a pit of regret about how everything you do in life is inevitably wrong. You'll question the tone of your last text message, wondering if you came across too eager, too distant, or too sarcastic. Suddenly, you're deep in the weeds, reflecting on your entire social life. This is just the beginning, my friend.

Smaller concerns will eventually evolve into larger concerns. You want to really focus on the fact that you always have something to worry about. This should be relatively easy if you follow the steps in chapter 4.

Procrastination is best for increasing misery if you only worry about things when you should be resting.

Step 3: Move from Minor Concerns to Global Catastrophes

Now that you've sufficiently overthought the small stuff, it's time to take your thoughts to the next level. This is when the real magic happens. Your brain, looking for something bigger and scarier, will naturally move from the mundane to the catastrophic. You'll start wondering about your future—or worse, your past.

Was that one decision you made in 2012 the reason you're still single? What if you chose a different college? What if you took that job offer instead of staying in your current position, which you now hate with a passion? And just like that, you're not thinking about your lunch order anymore. You're thinking about your *entire life* and how it's all a series of missed opportunities.

And this is when the global catastrophes come in. Global warming, the rise of AI, the decline of civilization, and your ever-present fear of being part of a generation that will never truly accomplish anything. What's the point of trying if the world is just going to end in 20 years? Or maybe it's 50? Who even knows anymore?

Step 4: Make It Personal—The Soul-Searching Interrogation

By now, you've been questioning everything in your life. You've analyzed your career, your relationships, your social media presence, and your tendency to cancel plans. But it's time to go deeper. It's time for a full-blown, 3 AM soul-searching session.

"Why am I even here?" you'll ask yourself. "Am I doing what I'm *meant* to be doing? Or am I just floating through life, hoping I can make it to the end without anyone noticing how little I've achieved?" You'll question your entire existence, trying to figure out if your contributions to society are meaningful or if you're just another cog in the machine.

Of course, you'll ignore the fact that most of the world is asleep, living out their quiet, functional lives, because your focus is now entirely on the fact that YOU are awake, contemplating the meaning of life in your bed, all alone.

go through every major decision you've ever made and then unravel every minor one. "Should I have gone to therapy sooner? Did I waste years in a job I hated? Did I even need to go to college? Am I just chasing the wrong dreams because I'm terrified of failure?" And then it hits you—*Is this all there is to life?*

Step 5: Dwell on Everything You'll Never Achieve

By now, you've spent hours (or what feels like hours) thinking about every unachieved goal you've ever had. All the things you could have done but didn't. The career that never took off. The half-finished novel gathering dust on your computer. The dream body you'll never have. The friends you've neglected because you were too busy binge-watching yet another series. The side hustle you abandoned for no reason. And as the spiral deepens, you'll start feeling the full weight of everything you've never done and the crushing realization that there's still time left to fail spectacularly.

It's at this point that your brain decides to present you with your deepest fear: what if you never reach your potential? What if the dream of a fulfilling life is nothing but an illusion, a story we tell ourselves to cope with the crushing weight of our own mediocrity? But don't worry—this is normal. It's just part of the process. The darker, more self-reflective thoughts are what turn the 3 AM spiral into a full-on existential crisis.

Reflection

The 3 AM spiral is an art, and if you've made it this far, you've undoubtedly perfected the process. There's no need to worry, though—this is just part of the human experience. While others sleep soundly, you'll always have the privilege of contemplating the vast mysteries of the universe from the comfort of your own bed. Just remember, when all else fails, there's always tomorrow to spiral again. So why not make tonight the perfect opportunity to embrace the chaos of your own mind?

Chapter 6: Turning Molehills into Mountains: An Expert's Guide to Catastrophizing

At some point, you'll try to reassure yourself. Maybe you'll tell yourself, "It's okay. I'll figure it out tomorrow." But that's a lie. Because by now, you're so deep in the spiral that no rational thought will pull you out. The self-reassurance is just a fleeting moment of calm before the next wave of catastrophic thinking hits. By the time the sun rises and your alarm goes off, you'll be a shell of a person, already regretting staying up and considering how little sleep you've gotten. But hey, that's the beauty of the 3 AM spiral—sleep is for the functional, and you, my friend, are anything but.

Step 1: Assume the Worst-Case Scenario

Anxiety should be the driving force for nearly every decision you make if you want to be miserable. That little voice in the back of your head that will tell you everything is fine; you need to do everything in your power to silence it. Everything is an example of a potential catastrophe if you simply think about it hard enough.

Did you send a typo in an email? Clearly, your boss now thinks you're incompetent and is drafting your termination letter. Always leap to the most extreme and unlikely conclusion—it's the cornerstone of catastrophizing.

Step 2: Stack Your Worries

A combination of problems can be your biggest downfall. Remember that everything is a disaster. And everything should feel like they are pilling up. Try to ignore any good things that happen in your day.

Don't stop at one problem. Let's say you spilled coffee on your shirt. Now you're late, you'll miss the meeting, your career is over, and you'll end up living under a bridge. Stack each worry on top of the last until your original issue feels like the least of your concerns.

The cumulative effect is what you want. It should feel like death from a thousand cuts from every issue seemingly piling up. If you pile up your worries enough, even the most minor thing can feel the end of the world.

Step 3: Turn Minor Setbacks into Personal Failures

Forget that everyone makes mistakes. If something goes wrong, it's clear because you're fundamentally flawed. You are the reason why everything bad happens to you. And you need to be striving for perfection. Or, at least what you think perfection is.

Didn't finish your to-do list? Proof that you'll never succeed at anything. Stuck in traffic? The universe is obviously out to get you. Have friends not spoken to you in a while? It's probably because they just find you to be annoying. You probably are annoying.

It helps if you can find the link to why you are the singular cause to a problem. And even if someone else is the cause of your problem, you should still think of yourself as the problem for even trusting someone else. You really want to set yourself up as the bad guy in your own story.

Step 4: Fixate on Things You Can't Control

Now that you are blaming yourself for things you can control, let's focus on things you can't control. You know you can't control everything, but that shouldn't avert your focus. Negative mindsets require constant focus on negative things. Luckily for you, most things can be considered out of your control. And there is no shortage of negative things out of your control.

Is your favorite television show cancelled? Perfect. Spend hours lamenting how unfair the entertainment industry is. Got caught in the rain without an umbrella? Don't just accept it—fume about how meteorologists failed you. The more powerless you feel, the better.

Step 5: Exaggerate the Consequences

Bob Marley's famous song quotes, "Don't worry, about a thing. Because every little thing is gonna be alright." In actually, most things will only be some minor in consequence. But that shouldn't stop you. Every consequence is the end of the world with enough practice.

When your friend doesn't text back immediately, assume they're mad at you. But don't stop there! Imagine the fallout: you'll lose the friendship, become a social pariah, and spend the rest of your days alone. Isn't overreacting fun?

It's a practice in being dramatic. Blowing things out of proportion to the breaking point. Thinking of the consequence over and over until it feels larger than it actually it. Only a mature person would be willing to move past something. You are better than being mature. You're immature.

Step 6: Practice Mental Time Travel

Why only focus on the present and the future? You have an entire lifetime of experience to draw negativity from. Thinking throughout your life, you can always find something that is bad. Actually, your brain is hard wired to remember bad things. You're just leaning into that mental habit.

Revisit every embarrassing thing you've ever done and relive the humiliation in vivid detail. Then fast-forward to your imagined future failures. This way, you can ruin both your past and future at the same time!

Step 7: Compare Your Struggles to Everyone Else's Successes

Why stop at your own problems? Look around and notice how everyone else seems to have their lives together. You never really get to see them go through anything bad. Clearly, they've never faced a single obstacle, and your issues are uniquely insurmountable.

This is an exercise in comparing yourself to avoid nuance in other people's lives. You really want to prevent conversations with other people when they talk about their problems. The key is denial of the situation. You are going through a hard time, so you must be the only one.

Step 8: Seek Validation from the Wrong People

I know that up until now, you probably thought I was going to tell you to avoid talking to people about your problems. That's such a rookie mistake. Truly miserable people constantly remind other people about their problems. They just use a very special technique.

Share your worries with someone who'll either dismiss them or add fuel to the fire. *"Oh, you're worried about your presentation? Yeah, public speaking ruins careers all the time."* The more unhelpful their response, the better for your catastrophizing streak.

People will try to give you the advice if they care. Most people cannot solve your problems for you. Their advice will be too general. This makes it easy to dismiss their ability to help you. You can also use thigs as proof that you are seeking help, it's just that nobody knows what to do in your situation.

Step 9: Avoid Solutions at All Costs

Problem solving is the most mentally healthy thing you can do. Why solve a problem when you can obsess over it instead? Solutions are for optimists. True catastrophizers know that real satisfaction comes from wallowing in the enormity of a problem without ever addressing it.

Take, for example, an issue with a friend, spouse, or job. You can try to work through your issues, but why? That would just lead to a resolution in the conflict.

You should instead wallow in your self-pity that you are even going through the problem. Use that complaining as nothing more than a minor release.

Step 10: Repeat Until Exhausted

Catastrophizing is a full-time commitment. Keep spiraling until you're emotionally drained and incapable of functioning. Life will be a bleak thing that you will have a hard time looking forward to. And you will often struggle with it by finding healthy relationships.

You should repeat these steps until one of two things happens with your relationships. The first is that people just avoid talking to you because you do nothing but drag them down. The second is that you manage to drag them down with you.

Both are pretty good options for being a horribly toxic person. But the second is preferable. Other people who are overly negative around you can reinforce your own negativity. Giving you long term dividends towards you self-destruction. Your group can even define themselves as the negative group. Just another personality trait that disguises mental illness.

By following these steps, you can turn even the smallest inconvenience into a monumental crisis. After all, life is too short to stay calm and rational. Coming up next: "Burning Bridges: A Hobby for the Chronically Discontent."

Chapter 7: Burning Bridges: A Hobby for the Chronically Discontent

Why let relationships linger when you can torch them in spectacular fashion? Burning bridges isn't just an impulsive act—it's a lifestyle choice. In this chapter, we'll guide you through the process of severing ties with friends, coworkers, and loved ones in ways so dramatic, you'll be remembered for years… and not in a good way.

Step 1: Assume the Worst Intentions

In life, there are various reasons why people do things. And sometimes, people will do things that aren't always the best for you. People will try to tell you that you shouldn't always assume the worst in other people's actions. Those people are losers.

Life is a never-ending game of chess. Every move someone makes is trying to checkmate you. They have their reasons, and those reasons aren't for you. At least, that's what you should tell yourself if you want to be miserable.

Did your friend cancel plans? Clearly, they hate you and have been plotting your downfall for years. Forget context or reasonable explanations—always jump to the most catastrophic conclusion. Paranoia is your best friend here.

Step 2: Overreact to Minor Conflicts

Now that you can assume the worst in everyone, it's time to act accordingly. People wronging you only should warrant you having a hostile reaction back. You need to dominate the issue by being the one who overreacts.

Someone forgot to text you back? Time to write a scathing message and hit send without thinking. Why resolve misunderstandings when you can escalate them into full-blown drama? Remember, it's not a true bridge-burning unless there's no chance of rebuilding.

Step 3: Gossip Like It's Your Job

Everyone's business is your business. Especially if it can be used to make relationships with people worse. Become the social network in real life. Become the person that everyone can go to for all the dirty laundry.

Share every negative thought you've ever had about someone with anyone who will listen. Bonus points if it gets back to the person you're talking about. After all, why keep grievances private when you can create a public spectacle?

Talking about other people's business is considered by many to be rude, inconsiderate, and just not helpful. You can just assume that those people have something to hide. That should only drive you toward finding out what they are hiding even more. This way, you are the center of attention while not being the center of gossip. Constantly diverting people to other people's problems.

Step 4: Bring Up Old Grudges

Moving on is for normal people. A truly miserable person never moves on from old problems. Why grow and work through your issues with others when you can forever be mad at them? The older the grudge, the better for stoking that fire.

Got a friend who forgot your birthday three years ago? Now's the perfect time to remind them. Dig up every slight, real or imagined, and throw it in their face during an argument. The more irrelevant the grudge, the better.

Step 5: Quit Your Job in Dramatic Fashion

Why leave your job in a mature fashion that would give you a god recommendation to your next job? We're here to burn bridges, not maintain connections. You need to be the center of attention when you leave your job. The star of the show that will have people talking about you for, maybe a few days at best.

Why submit a polite resignation letter when you can storm out in a blaze of glory? Send an all-staff email detailing every grievance you've ever had. Bonus points if you leave a passive-aggressive note on your boss's desk.

Your feelings and grudges are more important than your career. Remember that everything is everyone else's fault. And nothing is your own.

Step 6: Ignore Basic Communication

Connection is the most important thing to maintain relationships. We aren't here to do that. We're here to sabotage them. And you need to go out of your way to ignore the people closest to you. Ghosting isn't just for dating apps.

Stop responding to texts, emails, or calls from people you care about. When they finally confront you, act offended that they're even reaching out. You should bring up the fact that you really want privacy. Even after you constantly complain to them about your problems. Emotional whiplash is key.

Step 7: Make Everything About You

Being a miserable person takes a lot of one-sided communication. You need to constantly air out your problems to the people around you. People will try to open up to you. You need to shut that down fast before you end up having healthy communication.

If a friend is going through a tough time, remind them how inconvenient their struggles are for you. When they call you out, accuse them of being selfish. Nothing burns a bridge faster than unchecked narcissism.

Step 8: Sabotage Group Activities

Be the person that just ruins everything for everyone else. This is called being a stick in the mud. Finding out how you can ruin things can be pretty tricky. Here are a few examples.

Organizing a group trip or project? Perfect. Show up late, criticize everyone's ideas, and contribute as little as possible. Does everyone want to go to the beach? Show up without any beach equipment, and complain that you don't like sand. When the group inevitably falls apart, blame everyone else for the failure.

You are actively trying to avoid having any fun with your social gatherings. Even though you voluntarily went with them, that doesn't mean they can't cater to you. Staying stubborn in your problems with gathering is a great way to keep your friends and family away from you.

Step 9: Publicly Air Your Grievances

No problem is too small for you to mention. No stage is too small or big for your complaints. You need to be the complainer. Tell everyone about every complaint that you have. No matter how small, people need to hear it.

Social media is your stage, and petty drama is your script. Post vague, passive-aggressive statuses about people you're upset with. Tag them if you're feeling especially bold. The goal is maximum exposure and minimum resolution.

Step 10: Burn Bridges with Yourself

Finally, don't forget to alienate the most important person in your life: yourself. Become your own worst critic, your harshest judge, and your most relentless enemy. Self-sabotage any goals you set, preferably before you even start working on them—it's not failure if you never tried, right? Ignore your needs entirely; who needs rest, nourishment, or a little kindness when you can replace them with self-inflicted guilt and shame?

Who needs external enemies when you've got yourself? Truly, the best battles are fought—and lost—internally.

By mastering the art of burning bridges, you'll ensure that your life remains filled with drama, isolation, and regret. But don't worry—there are always new bridges to burn! Coming up next: "Faking it Till you Break it: How to Avoid Therapy"

Chapter 8: Faking It Till You Break It: How to Avoid Therapy

Therapy is for people who *admit* they have problems. But you? You're way too good at pretending everything is fine. Sure, your mental health is a ticking time bomb, but why acknowledge that when you can keep up the facade of having it all together until everything falls apart spectacularly? This chapter will teach you how to avoid therapy at all costs and maintain the illusion that you're thriving, even if you're one step away from an emotional meltdown.

Step 1: Master the "I'm Fine" Face

If there's one phrase you must master in this life, it's "I'm fine." Not "okay," not "good," but the all-important, "I'm fine." Perfecting this phrase is an art form. You need to say it with a smile that's just a little too wide and a tone that's slightly too high-pitched to make anyone believe it.

Practice in the mirror for maximum effect. Bonus points if you can add a quick subject change—because nothing says "I've got this under control" like a sudden shift to the weather. Everyone will buy it, and you'll avoid any probing questions about your obvious downward spiral.

Step 2: Smile Like You're Winning at Life

You're not winning at life. In fact, life is probably winning at you. But no one needs to know that. Every time you walk into a room, throw on your best "I'm successful, I'm content, and I've definitely got my emotional baggage packed away in a sealed, undisclosed location" smile. If you can't muster genuine joy, go for exaggerated enthusiasm.

You're basically an emotional circus performer at this point, and it's all for show. The more cheerful and upbeat you look, the less anyone will bother you with their concerns. Smile like a robot that's been programmed to be optimistic, and keep those red flags buried beneath a layer of confidence.

Step 3: Avoid Deep Conversations Like the Plague

If someone dares to venture beyond surface-level chitchat, redirect, deflect, and escape. The goal is to keep conversations light and shallow, never straying into the emotional waters where your own vulnerability might drown you.

If they ask how you're really doing, hit them with a casual, "Oh, you know, life, am I right?" and immediately bring up an irrelevant topic—like your cat's latest antics or a minor inconvenience, like a broken nail. The key here is to shut down any real emotional exchange before it even starts. You'll come off as an enigma—mysterious, composed, and definitely not spiraling.

Step 4: Take on More Than You Can Handle

When people offer help or ask if you need anything, your instinct should be to say "yes" to everything, regardless of how impossible or overwhelming it is. You're not allowed to admit you can't handle it.

Overwhelm yourself with tasks, responsibilities, and commitments, because who needs personal boundaries when you're juggling a self-imposed hurricane of stress? Remember, the more you pile onto your plate, the better you'll look when you eventually crumble. The shock and awe will make your eventual breakdown that much more satisfying.

Step 5: Suppress, Suppress, Suppress

Emotions? Who needs them? Instead of dealing with your feelings, suppress them with the skill of a seasoned professional. Every time you feel an emotion rising up, stuff it down into your soul like it's an unwanted inheritance. Crying? Not in your vocabulary. Anger?

Who, you? Forget about it. Anxiety? Just a figment of your imagination. As you bottle up every uncomfortable feeling, you'll build a beautiful, slowly expanding volcano of emotional dysfunction that will erupt at the most inconvenient moment. The louder the eruption, the more dramatic your meltdown will be, so suppress away—your emotional explosion will be worth it when it finally comes.

Step 6: Practice Self-Diagnosis (But Only the Fun Ones)

Why go to therapy when you can self-diagnose on the internet? There are hundreds of free quizzes online that can tell you exactly what's wrong with you, all without the discomfort of actually talking to a licensed professional.

Diagnose yourself with things like "chronic sarcasm," "existential dread," or "acute burnout," and make sure to tell everyone that you've got it *all figured out*. After all, you're a DIY psychologist with a wealth of Google searches under your belt. You don't need a therapist—what you need is a really good meme that speaks to your soul.

Step 7: Treat Your Mental Health Like a Bad Habit

Avoid looking at your mental health like it's a serious issue. It's just a little phase, a quirky part of your personality that you can ignore. After all, who needs therapy when you have a Netflix subscription and an endless supply of snacks? Treat your mental health like a bad habit that will eventually work itself out. Procrastinate therapy until the feelings become so overwhelming that you can no longer avoid the inevitable. Only then will you realize that pretending everything was fine was just an elaborate game of emotional Jenga—and your tower is about to come crashing down.

Step 8: Wait for the Implosion

After months or years of pretending everything is fine, it's time to let it all fall apart in one magnificent spectacle. You'll reach a point where you can no longer hold it together, and all the little cracks you've ignored will burst open in a glorious emotional explosion. When that happens, make sure to do it in a public setting, preferably somewhere inconvenient, like a friend's wedding or your workplace's annual meeting. You've earned this moment of pure, unfiltered chaos. Let it all out. It's the only thing you've done with any honesty for a while.

Reflection

Faking it is an art, but it's also exhausting. By avoiding therapy and pretending to have it all under control, you're not just denying yourself the chance to heal; you're also setting yourself up for a colossal meltdown. So, remember—keep smiling, keep overloading your schedule, and keep suppressing your emotions. But when everything inevitably implodes, you'll finally have a good story to tell... just after you've picked up the pieces of your shattered life.

Chapter 9: Money Can't Buy Happiness, But Debt Can Buy Misery

Everyone says money can't buy happiness, but have you ever tried mismanaging your finances? If you really want to embrace true misery, there's no better way than plunging yourself into debt. This chapter will provide you with all the essential financial mismanagement tips to ensure that your wallet is as emotionally bankrupt as your self-esteem.

Step 1: Spend First, Think Later

Why save money for the future when you can live in the moment? If you've ever found yourself thinking, *"I'll figure it out later"* after maxing out your credit card on a shopping spree, then you're already on the right path. Always prioritize immediate gratification over long-term financial security.

If you don't have the cash, just put it on a credit card, because what could go wrong? It's only a matter of time before the bills catch up with you, but by then, you'll have a mountain of stuff you definitely don't need to distract you. Plus, worrying about payments is a great way to keep that "low-level anxiety" going strong.

Step 2: Forget About Budgeting

Budgeting is for people who want to know where their money is going. And let's be honest—who really wants to live like that? If you've ever sat down to track your spending and felt your soul leave your body, you're doing it right. Instead of budgeting, just rely on your *vibes*. If you feel like spending $300 on impulse purchases during a weekend trip, then go for it. When it comes time to check your bank account and see what you've got left, simply ignore it. Who needs financial planning when you've got dreams and credit cards?

Step 3: Take Out Loans for Fun Stuff

A student loan? Boring. A car loan? Yawn. If you're going to borrow money, do it for something truly special. Need a new phone every six months, or a 60-inch TV you'll never actually watch? Take out a loan for that. Consider this an investment in your *immediate* happiness. The interest rates might not make you happy, but that's the price of living lavishly on borrowed time. The best part? You get to feel a little thrill every time you check your balance and realize just how deep in debt you've become.

Step 4: Skip the Emergency Fund, Embrace the Panic

Who needs an emergency fund when life is *fine*? Instead of putting aside money for unexpected expenses, take pride in living paycheck to paycheck. This way, when the car breaks down or you need an emergency root canal, you'll get to experience the full, heart-pounding joy of scrambling to figure out how you'll pay for it.

The thrill of uncertainty is unmatched—every unexpected expense is like a game of financial roulette, and you're just hoping that the wheel lands on something you can at least *half* afford.

Step 5: Ignore Your Credit Score

What's the point of worrying about your credit score when it's so much more fun to ignore it? Late fees? Overdue payments? Just let them pile up. Every missed payment is a step closer to achieving the *perfect* financial disaster. Think of it as a badge of honor. The higher your debt, the more elusive your credit score becomes, and that's really the best kind of freedom, right?

Forget about future loans, mortgages, or the possibility of ever owning a house—your current moment of stress and debt is all that matters.

Step 6: Only Buy Things That Are *On Sale*

A sale is your best friend. Why pay full price when you can buy three items you don't need for the price of one? Sales, discounts, and "limited time offers" are the perfect excuse to fill your cart with unnecessary items. Sure, you might not have any actual money for groceries, but who needs food when you've got 15 t-shirts and two blenders you'll never use?

Overconsumption is not only financially irresponsible, but also a fantastic way to inflate your self-worth in the short term. You can replace any negative feeling about yourself with the thrill of buying things. It's better than therapy. Remember, if you can't afford it, just put it on layaway!

Step 7: Avoid Financial Advice Like the Plague

Financial advisors are just people who want to ruin your fun. Who needs boring things like debt-to-income ratios and retirement plans when you could be living your life to the fullest—*right now*? Avoid reading any articles about budgeting, saving, or investing.

That's just *future-you's* problem. Instead, focus on how you can spend all your money now, because the future is overrated. When people talk about saving for retirement, nod politely and then change the subject to something more fun—like how much you spent on your latest impulse buy.

Step 8: Make Sure to Max Out Your Credit Cards

The goal is to reach your credit card limit as quickly as possible. If you're not maxing out your credit cards on unnecessary purchases, then what are you even doing? You *have* to be living on the edge. When you hit your limit, that's when the real fun begins—waiting to see when your next payment will come due and wondering if you'll be able to juggle the bills. The real thrill is in knowing that you're one small financial misstep away from total ruin.

Step 9: Embrace the "I'll Deal with It Later" Mindset

The beauty of financial mismanagement is in procrastination. Don't pay your bills on time? Just push it to the back of your mind. Max out your credit cards? Don't worry about it until your creditors come knocking. Future you can handle it, right? Besides, who needs to worry about something so small when you've got a mountain of stress and late fees to look forward to? The "I'll deal with it later" mindset is truly an art form. You're living in the now, even if that now is a financial nightmare.

Reflection

So, you've taken all the right steps to ensure your financial misery. By overspending, avoiding budgeting, and embracing debt, you've achieved the pinnacle of financial dysfunction. But here's the catch: this path, while full of brief, chaotic satisfaction, will eventually lead to a *hilarious* reckoning. When the bill collectors start calling, the debt collectors show up at your door, and your credit score is lower than your self-esteem, you'll realize that maybe—just maybe—financial stability isn't so overrated after all.

Until then, keep spending! Just don't ask for a loan when you inevitably need therapy to deal with the chaos you've created.

Chapter 10: Life Without Goals: A Path to Glorious Stagnation

Some people say you need goals to succeed in life. Those people are probably *busy*, and honestly, that sounds exhausting. If you're ready to embrace true inner peace—one that comes with the blissful surrender of ambition—this chapter is for you. Here, we will celebrate the art of aimlessness, avoid any and all forms of goal-setting, and strive for the most serene state of existence: stagnation. Because, really, who needs to move forward when you could just... not?

Step 1: Banish the Word "Ambition" from Your Vocabulary

Ambition is for people who want things, and things are overrated. The first step to living a goal-free life is to eliminate the very concept of *wanting* something. From now on, when someone asks you about your dreams, shrug and respond with, "I mean, why bother?"

Then, proceed to change the subject to something utterly unambitious, like your plans to re-watch *The Office* for the fifteenth time. Every time the word "ambition" enters a conversation, remind everyone that you're *just here for the ride*—no plans, no pressure, just existing.

Step 2: Keep Your To-Do Lists as Vague as Possible

To-do lists are for people who want to feel productive, and productivity is for the weak. Your to-do list should consist of the most general, non-committal tasks, such as "Think about doing laundry" or "Contemplate future plans." Never write down anything with a definitive deadline or specific steps.

If you're feeling particularly ambitious (which you shouldn't be), add tasks like "Vaguely consider a new hobby" or "Check in on friends, but don't make plans." The beauty of vague to-do lists is that they never burden you with the need to actually accomplish anything—just the satisfaction of *thinking about it.*

Step 3: Avoid Long-Term Planning Like the Plague

Planning for the future is a quick ticket to stress, so it's best to just skip it entirely. Why bother with saving for retirement, buying a home, or setting up a career plan when you can simply drift through life without any destination in mind? The key to glorious stagnation is to live only in the present moment—and even that can be overrated sometimes. Keep your future plans as blurry as possible. When someone asks where you see yourself in five years, respond with, "I don't know, maybe still binge-watching this show… who can say?" That way, you avoid the suffocating pressure of having to achieve anything substantial.

Step 4: Master the Art of the Unfinished Project

Nothing says "I'm living my best, most unstressed life" like a room full of half-started projects. Whether it's an art project, a self-improvement book you bought three years ago, or a fitness routine you started once and immediately abandoned, leave these projects hanging. The point isn't to finish; it's to *start* things and then comfortably forget about them.

Every unfinished endeavor is a monument to your commitment to aimlessness. At best, it will provide a small, fleeting sense of accomplishment before you inevitably lose interest and move on to something else (or, preferably, nothing at all).

Step 5: Embrace the Joy of Being "Busy Doing Nothing"

In the world of ambitious go-getters, there's something truly revolutionary about doing absolutely nothing. The key to a blissful existence without goals is to prioritize leisure over labor. Spend entire afternoons sitting in a comfortable chair and staring out the window. Contemplate the deep mysteries of life, such as why you can never seem comfortable, or whether socks truly do disappear in the dryer.

It's not a waste of time; it's *finding peace* in stagnation. If anyone questions your inactivity, simply tell them that you're "recharging"—after all, personal growth can only be achieved through hours of intentional, goal-free relaxation.

Step 6: Say "No" to Self-Improvement

Self-improvement is for people who think there's something wrong with them, which is frankly absurd. Why fix what isn't broken? If you've ever bought a self-help book or considered taking a course on productivity, *stop right now*. The goal here is to reject any notion that you can or should improve yourself. Instead, embrace the art of *being fine with how you are*. Let the world's obsession with betterment pass you by.

Don't read books that promise you'll "unlock your full potential" or "become your best self"—the best self is one that exists without pressure, deadlines, or growth. *You are already perfect*, just as you are… aimless.

Step 7: Fill Your Calendar with Absolutely Nothing

Calendars are for people who believe in the illusion of control. If you're aiming for stagnation, you must embrace the beauty of empty days. Never schedule anything that requires effort or engagement. If you need to put something down on the calendar, make it something that will only take up a fraction of your energy, like "watch an entire season of reality TV" or "take a nap in the middle of the day."

The key is to ensure that there's always an abundance of unstructured time available for you to do nothing. If someone asks about your plans, reply with the vague yet satisfying "Nothing special—just seeing where the day takes me."

Step 8: Let Regret Be Your Guide

Regret can be a powerful force if you let it. Instead of setting goals and striving for success, lean into the sweet sorrow of unfulfilled potential. Let the lack of progress become the only progress you need.

The absence of achievement will serve as a constant reminder of the freedom you have from the tyranny of ambition. When people ask if you're planning to do something about your *lack* of a goal-oriented life, give them a look that says, "I've already done enough—nothing."

Reflection

Living a life without goals isn't a defeat—it's an art form. It's about giving up the constant pressure of achievement, ignoring the expectations of others, and finding comfort in the stillness of stagnation. The truly ambitious person doesn't climb mountains—they sit at the base and enjoy the view without the need to conquer anything. And if you happen to get bored with that, well… it's probably time to *re-watch the same show again.* The point is to never rush. After all, what's the point of getting somewhere when you can enjoy the bliss of being nowhere?

Chapter 11: Why Hope Is Dangerous: Stay Cynical, Stay Safe

Hope is a dangerous thing. People talk about it like it's some kind of lifeline, but really, it's more like a trap—a cruel joke the universe plays on the hopeful. If you want to maintain your mental well-being and avoid unnecessary disappointment, this chapter will teach you the valuable skill of keeping your expectations as low as your serotonin levels. Because the lower you set the bar, the fewer times it will hurt when you fail to jump over it.

Step 1: Embrace the Eternal Darkness of Realism

Let's get one thing straight: optimism is a lie. When someone says, "Look on the bright side," they're either lying to themselves or trying to sell you something.

Realism, on the other hand, is about accepting the truth of what is—and the truth is, life is mostly mediocre with a few minor disasters thrown in.

Instead of wishing for the impossible or dreaming of success, focus on the bare minimum. Expect the worst. And when the worst happens, you'll be pleasantly surprised (or at least not as devastated). Forget about imagining things getting better; it's safer to assume they won't.

Step 2: Lower Your Standards to the Basement

Hope thrives on high standards—standards that are often unattainable and unrealistic. Your goal should be to reduce your standards to something so low that they don't even touch the floor. The lower your expectations, the fewer ways life can disappoint you. You don't need a promotion; just showing up to work every day is victory enough.

You don't need a perfect relationship; any mutual disinterest in each other's presence will do. Your friends don't need to be there for you—just remember their names when you see them at the grocery store.

Step 3: Master the Art of Preemptive Disappointment

Why wait for life to disappoint you when you can do it to yourself in advance? Preemptive disappointment is the key to emotional protection. The next time someone tells you they'll "definitely" make plans with you, just assume they won't. When a friend talks about their big dreams, nod politely, but mentally prepare yourself for the inevitable crash when those dreams go unfulfilled.

Hope only leaves you vulnerable, but with preemptive disappointment, you're ready for whatever comes—or, more accurately, *doesn't* come. The best part? You won't feel a thing when the inevitable disappointment lands because you were already "over it."

Step 4: Assume Everything Will Go Wrong

When you assume everything will go wrong, you're never caught off guard. That movie you've been wanting to see? It'll probably be a flop. That vacation you've been planning? Expect a hurricane or a plague of locusts. The new relationship you're starting?

They're likely to be a complicated disaster who refuses to communicate, and you'll never get the closure you need. This mindset isn't pessimism; it's just preparing for the worst with the quiet satisfaction that, if it all turns out fine, you'll be pleasantly surprised. But if it doesn't, you can sigh dramatically and say, "Well, I knew that was coming."

Step 5: Don't Let Anyone Else's Positivity Ruin Your Mood

Some people will try to drag you into their little world of sunny optimism. They'll tell you that anything is possible and that if you just try hard enough, you can achieve your wildest dreams. These people are a menace. Politely smile and let their toxic positivity wash over you without absorbing it.

You're not falling for that trap. You can still be happy for others' success while keeping your expectations firmly grounded in reality. Let them reach for the stars while you enjoy your very comfortable place on the ground, far from the stress of those elusive constellations.

Step 6: Stop Worrying About the Future—It's All Overrated

The future? It's a big question mark, and honestly, who cares? When people talk about "planning for the future," just smile and nod, then go back to your life of delightful, blissful stagnation. Forget about retirement accounts, career goals, or being a better person in five years. The future is a concept invented by people with too much time on their hands.

The truth is, the future will arrive whether you worry about it or not, and it's unlikely to be any better than today. When in doubt, invest your time in the now: Avoid long-term plans, don't set any big dreams, and simply exist.

Step 7: Hope is Just Another Way to Be Disappointed

The problem with hope is that it opens the door to disappointment. If you hope for something—say, a job promotion, the perfect partner, or even just an uneventful week—you set yourself up for a fall. And when that fall inevitably happens, you'll be crushed by the weight of your unmet expectations.

It's better to assume nothing good will happen, so when it does, you can sit back and enjoy the pleasant surprise. But let's be honest, it's not likely that much will change. The best strategy? Get comfortable with the idea that you'll probably never get what you hope for, and then, when you don't, you'll be oddly satisfied by how right you were.

Step 8: Practice the "Whatever" Philosophy

Why care? It's an easy mantra, and it's incredibly effective. When something mildly exciting happens, simply shrug and say, "Whatever." The more you train yourself to downplay everything, the less you'll ever be let down.

Sure, you could get excited about that new project at work or that concert you're attending, but chances are, it'll fall through or be underwhelming. By not allowing yourself to get caught up in hope, you save yourself the emotional rollercoaster of disappointment. If you're ever tempted to hope, just remind yourself: "Whatever. It probably won't work out."

Reflection

The world will always try to sell you hope as a cure for life's many ills. But hope is nothing more than a band-aid, and the real solution is cynicism. When you lower your expectations and accept that everything will likely go wrong, you stop setting yourself up for heartache. There's no vulnerability in cynicism—just the peaceful calm of knowing that life won't surprise you, because you've already prepared for the worst. So, stay cynical. It's safer, it's easier, and it's remarkably peaceful when you stop hoping for things that will only let you down.

Chapter 12: Congratulations! You're Your Own Worst Enemy

You've made it to the final chapter. *You're still here,* which, frankly, is a small miracle considering how thoroughly you've sabotaged your own chances of success at every turn. But fear not, dear reader—you've achieved a level of self-sabotage that can only be described as artful. You've expertly thwarted your own potential and prevented any sort of progress from creeping into your life. In fact, you've become so skilled at being your own worst enemy that, in a way, you deserve a medal. So, congratulations. You are a master of self-destruction, and this final chapter will celebrate that skill and teach you how to weaponize it for maximum effect.

Step 1: Embrace Procrastination Like It's Your Best Friend

Procrastination is the key to avoiding any and all responsibility. If you truly want to sabotage your future, this is your secret weapon. The beauty of procrastination lies in its ability to turn simple tasks into enormous, unsolvable problems. Why do something today when you can put it off indefinitely?

Whether it's a work project, a personal goal, or even just getting out of bed, procrastination ensures that you're never quite in the position to achieve anything. And when the deadline looms and you're completely unprepared, you can delight in the glorious panic that only last-minute scrambling can provide. Procrastination is your ally, and it will always be there when you need an excuse to do nothing.

Step 2: Let Self-Doubt Be Your Inner Voice

Nothing kills potential like self-doubt, and no one does it better than you. Every time you feel the slightest bit of optimism about an idea or plan, let that voice in your head remind you that you're not good enough. "You don't deserve that promotion," "People will laugh at your idea," "You're not capable of anything,"—these are the thoughts that will keep you safely ensnared in the trap of mediocrity.

The more you doubt yourself, the less you'll ever attempt to reach higher, and thus, the less you'll fail— except when it comes to avoiding all the things that might actually improve your life. Keep feeding yourself these thoughts. You're really doing yourself a favor.

Step 3: Set Impossible Standards for Yourself

The quickest way to sabotage any attempt at success is to hold yourself to standards that no one, not even a superhuman, could ever meet. Aim to achieve things that are so ridiculously out of reach that, when you inevitably fall short, you can look back and say, "Well, I gave it my all, and that's just not enough." Set goals like "Become a billionaire by next year" or "Master a new language in one week."

The beauty of impossible standards is that they guarantee failure and provide endless opportunities for self-blame. It's the perfect way to ensure you'll never be content with what you achieve, even when you're doing just fine.

Step 4: Make Sure You're Always Distracted

To truly derail any chance of forward movement, surround yourself with distractions. Constantly check your phone. Start unnecessary side projects that will never get finished. Let every social media notification pull you away from anything remotely productive. The art of distraction is a finely honed skill—one that ensures your mind is always occupied with something *irrelevant*, making it impossible to focus on anything that might actually lead to growth or success.

Whether it's endless scrolling through memes or obsessing over someone else's opinion of you, distractions are the perfect way to avoid confronting any important issues. If you can't focus, you can't achieve anything—and that's the point.

Step 5: Commit to Emotional Rollercoasters

To ensure your emotional state is as unstable as possible, make sure to ride the emotional rollercoaster regularly. Let every setback, no matter how small, send you spiraling into a pit of despair. Let every minor win inflate your sense of accomplishment to a delusional high. That way, you can live in a state of constant emotional turmoil, preventing any semblance of balance or calm from entering your life.

Never allow yourself to be content for too long. After all, happiness is fleeting, and there's much more excitement in keeping yourself on the edge of a nervous breakdown. Your own mental chaos is the perfect way to avoid any kind of peace or stability.

Step 6: Never Take Responsibility for Your Actions

If you want to remain your own worst enemy, the last thing you should do is take responsibility for anything. Blame others for your failures, and never admit that your own actions might have contributed to your situation. The more you externalize your problems, the less likely you'll be to learn from them.

After all, if the problem is always someone else's fault, there's no need for self-reflection or change. Point fingers at your coworkers, your friends, your family— blame your circumstances, the weather, or the universe. It's always easier to play the victim than to take ownership of your own missteps.

Step 7: Push People Away with Perfectionism

Perfectionism is an excellent way to ensure that no one will ever want to work with you or be your friend. Set impossible standards for others, demand flawless results, and be deeply critical when things aren't done exactly as you envision them. If anyone challenges your perfectionist tendencies, push them away.

In fact, surround yourself with people who will never meet your expectations, then criticize them for not measuring up. Push them further and further away with your refusal to compromise or accept any level of imperfection. Eventually, you'll have the perfectly isolated life you've always wanted. And the best part? You'll get to do all the self-sabotaging alone.

Step 8: Keep Moving the Finish Line

One of the most brilliant ways to sabotage yourself is by constantly moving the finish line. If you ever do get close to achieving something, change the goal just before you reach it. Why settle for completing something when you could make it just a little bit harder? This way, you'll never experience the satisfaction of success because you've always made sure the end is just out of reach.

And when you *do* fail, you'll have the perfect excuse: you didn't try hard enough, or the goal was too lofty to begin with. Congratulations! You're guaranteed to stay in perpetual motion, never quite finishing anything, but always just one step away from something great.

Reflection

By now, you've mastered the art of self-sabotage. You've learned to procrastinate with grace, doubt yourself with flair, and hold yourself to standards that are impossible to meet. You've mastered the art of distraction and emotional chaos, all while refusing to take responsibility for your own actions. You've perfected the way to push people away, and you've learned to move the finish line just before you reach it. You're your own worst enemy, and you've earned that title. But don't worry—being your own worst enemy isn't a failure; it's a lifestyle. And now that you've embraced it, you can live comfortably in the knowledge that you'll never disappoint yourself with the burden of success.